How to BAKE a
UNIVERSE

HOW to BAKE a UNIVERSE

ALEC CARVLIN

Illustrated by
BRIAN BIGGS

Norton Young Readers
An Imprint of W. W. Norton & Company
Independent Publishers Since 1923

This book is dedicated to my parents, M&M, who brought me into this universe and taught me how incredible it can be.

And to F, who helped me realize it in this book.

—A.C.

For Sacha, my favorite baker.

—B.B.

For information about permission to reproduce selections from this book, write to Permissions, W. W. Norton & Company, Inc., 500 Fifth Avenue, New York, NY 10110

For information about special discounts for bulk purchases, please contact W. W. Norton Special Sales at specialsales@wwnorton.com or 800-233-4830

Manufacturing by Phoenix Color
Book design by Hana Anouk Nakamura
Production manager: Julia Druskin

Library of Congress Cataloging-in-Publication Data

Names: Carvlin, Alec, author. | Biggs, Brian, illustrator.
Title: How to bake a universe / Alec Carvlin ; illustrated by Brian Biggs.
Description: First edition. | New York : Norton Young Readers, an imprint of W.W. Norton, [2022]. | Audience: Ages 6–9.
Identifiers: LCCN 2021016613 | ISBN 9781324004233 (hardcover) | ISBN 9781324004240 (epub)
Subjects: LCSH: Cosmology—Juvenile literature. | Astrophysics—Juvenile literature. | Universe—Juvenile literature. | LCGFT: Picture books.
Classification: LCC QB983 .C374 2022 | DDC 523.01—dc23
LC record available at https://lccn.loc.gov/2021016613

W. W. Norton & Company, Inc., 500 Fifth Avenue, New York, N.Y. 10110
www.wwnorton.com

W. W. Norton & Company Ltd., 15 Carlisle Street, London W1D 3BS

0 9 8 7 6 5 4 3 2 1

To bake a universe,
you'll need a heaping pile of nothing.

That's right, not a single thing!

Just make sure you have enough.

If you're in need
of some nothing,
first look everywhere,

and then look nowhere.

Chances are you can
find some there.

When you're happy with your amount of nothing, gather it all up and pop it on a baking sheet.

Any size bigger than you can imagine will do—your universe will rise dramatically during baking.

Next, preheat your oven to Absolute Hot.

Keep in mind that everyone's oven is different, so if you don't see the Absolute Hot setting, that's okay. Just set it to Super Duper Really Very Mega Hot instead.

When your oven is preheated, you're ready to bake your universe! Or, almost ready. You just need one more thing . . .

Sunglasses: for style, protection, and close inspection. After all, you are making trillions of suns.

With your sunglasses in hand, you're ready. Say it out loud:

I'M READY!

Now carefully place the tray of nothing
on the center rack and step back.

There's going to be a big bang!

Not a big bang, silly—a Big Bang!

You won't hear anything or see anything, but rest assured, your universe is already the size of a balloon and inflating fast.

One trillionth of a trillionth of a trillionth
of a second later, turn your oven down a few
nonillion degrees, because things are about
to get . . .

. . . really very teeny tiny. Quarky, to be exact.

Quarky is not a word, you're right. But *quark* is! And right now, your universe is chock full of them . . . but not much else.

Want to take a peek?

Turn your oven light on, grab your magnifying glass, AND YOU WILL SEE . . .

Ha! Even the most powerful magnifying glass can't see quarks.

Luckily, this stuff you can't see is there only for a second. Seriously!

Only a second has passed since your universe started its journey from nothing to something, and more particles are on the way. Neat, huh?!

Wait another fraction of a second . . .

and voila!

Does your universe look like:

(a) a boily, bubbly soup?

(b) a topsy-turvy sea?

(c) a pond where all the fish are burping at once?

The correct answer is . . .

(d) all of the above!

And you're on the right track!

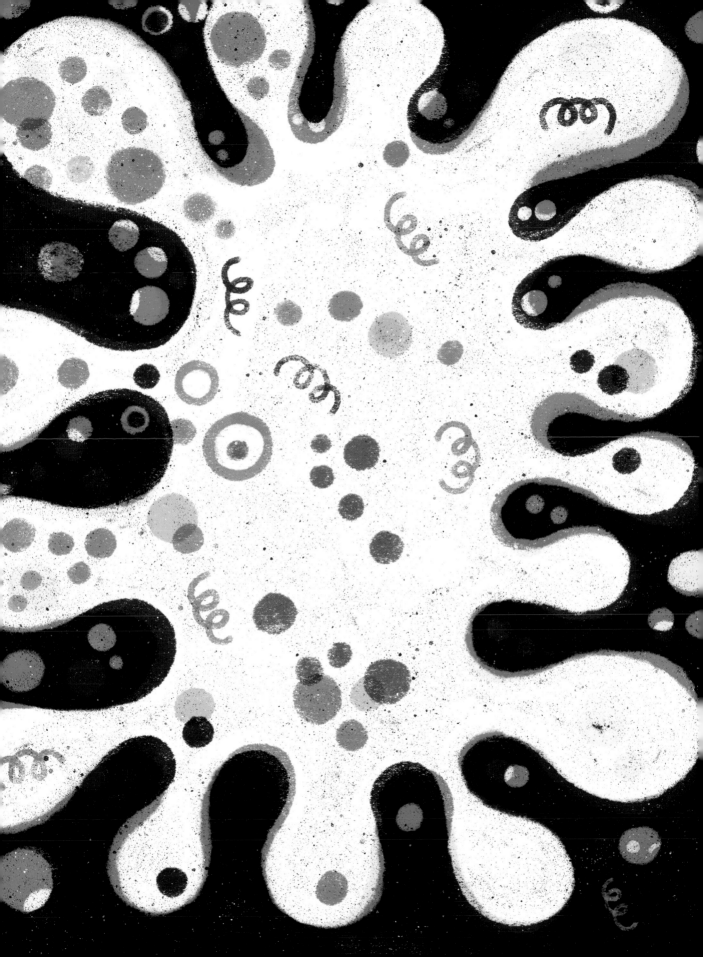

Now turn the temperature down to Just Sorta Kinda Hot and set the oven timer. Remember: you want your universe crisp, not burned. 377,000 years is probably good. That way, you'll have plenty of time to read a book and play outside while it bakes.

When the timer dings, turn off
the oven and watch closely.
That particle soup-sea-pond
is about to stop bubbling and
form atoms!

Actually, don't bother watching closely—you can't really see atoms, either. But you can think of them as extremely tiny building blocks that make much bigger stuff, like stars and planets.

Yes, exactly like Uranus, or Jupiter, or Mars.

But not yet.

Here's where your sunglasses come in.
Throw them on and grab your camera.
Don't worry, you won't need the flash.
Once your universe makes its first atoms,
there's going to be a big burst of—

Exactly. Tell your universe to say cheese!
That's all of your light escaping. It didn't
like being cooped up.

The picture will help scientists later when they want to know how it all began! You're making history, Chef—it's important to document it.

All that's left to do now is wait. Those atoms—mostly hydrogen and helium—will need some time to get to know one another. With a little convincing, though, they'll start to get nice and friendly. And gassy.

Not that kind of gassy.

Just set your timer for 180 million years. That will allow the gas clouds to come together and form scrumptious stars— without them, your universe would be as bland as a raw eggplant.

If you simply must have a taste test, though, waiting 179,999,999 years should be enough.

When time's up, head back into the kitchen.
Is your oven glowing? Perfect! That means
your stars are finally giving off light.

To make sure it's fully cooked, grab a toothpick and stick it in the center of your universe.

If gases come out, it needs more time. But if you pluck out a star, you're all set!

Now open the oven door and show off your universe!

Just be careful. Your universe has a lot of gravity, so keep a safe distance and ask an adult for help. You wouldn't want to fall in!

Or you could just summon your antigravity oven mitts. Go ahead, try it.

With your mitts fit snugly around your hands, take out the baking sheet and turn your universe upside-down onto the largest cooling rack you can find. Just a smidge smaller than infinity works every time.

Remove your oven mitts and wipe the sweat from your brow. It is not easy work, baking a universe.

Looks tasty doesn't it?

DON'T SERVE IT YET.

Universes are best experienced at room temperature, so you'll have to wait a little bit. About 13.6 billion years should do the trick.

That may seem like a long time to wait,
but there's plenty to see in the meantime.
Your stars will come together and form
swirly, spirally galaxies!

Planets will pop up and dance around!

And there will be explosions.

Big ones.

Once fully cooled, get out the frosting and sprinkles and . . . holy cosmic cannoli! Look around you! There's your universe, coming through the window, and there's your universe, hanging by the ceiling, and it's there and there and everywhere!

Hold on . . . *is* that your universe?

Or is it the kid's from next door?

Or is it the one from across the ocean?

Or the one aliens are baking in a galaxy far, far away?

This is the biggest test of all to see if your universe is ready. Can you tell your universe from your friend's, or your neighbor's, or those aliens'? If you answered "no" . . . YOU DID IT! IT'S DONE!

Because a universe isn't complete until it belongs to everyone.

So congratulations, Chef! Time to cut yourself a slice. It's going to be tough to choose, but don't worry about getting the perfect one. Every slice of the universe is the best slice.

How could it not be? It's ours.

Notes on the Text

you'll need a heaping pile of nothing There are many theories about how the universe began, one of which is that it simply started from a single point. This is called the Big Bang theory, and it is the most widely accepted origin model amongst astrophysicists and cosmologists. How something could actually start from nothing, though, remains a topic of debate.

Next, preheat your oven to Absolute Hot Absolute hot is a hypothetical temperature. Without a way of unifying Einstein's theory of general relativity with theories of quantum mechanics, knowing about these extremely high energy interactions and what they might mean is impossible. For our purposes here, Absolute Hot is a signpost that points to what the temperature might have been at the moment of the Big Bang. It could be infinitely hot, or it could be a number we can't know right now.

Not a big bang, silly—a Big Bang! The name "Big Bang" is misleading—it was not an explosion. It was the moment before all space expanded in every direction at once. Again, without a theory that unifies general relativity and quantum mechanics, it's impossible to know what exactly happened (and how) during the moment of the Big Bang. This is because it is, in a manner of speaking, a moment outside of space and time—the concepts on which Einstein based his theory of general relativity and our current understanding of gravity. Without a true understanding of spacetime at the smallest scales, we are unable to trace back to the exact moment of the Big Bang and understand all of the physics involved in that event.

your universe is already the size of a balloon and inflating fast Inflation is the moment immediately following the Big Bang, wherein the universe expanded rapidly in all directions at once. It is too hot for fundamental particles (such as quarks) to form, and all fundamental forces (gravity, electromagnetism, and the strong and weak forces) are thought to have been one force. Inflation is a tricky concept, as the universe wasn't expanding *into* anything. This is because the universe *is* everything. To say that anything exists beyond the universe is to contradict its very definition. Therefore, its inflation was into an ever-growing version of itself. For it to be the size of a balloon, as is referenced here, one would have had to stop the clock at around 10^{-35} seconds (an *unimaginably* tiny fraction of a second). Of course, this is only an estimate based on what we can observe of the universe today.

turn your oven down a few nonillion degrees This refers to the period after inflation when the universe had cooled enough to start forming fundamental particles, around 10^{-32} seconds after the Big Bang. The "nonillion" here is a matter of artistic license. Although scientists have been able to trace rough temperature estimates back to moments in the growth of the early universe, comparing any one of these moments to Absolute Hot (and whatever temperature that might be) is impossible. One could look at the difference in temperature between the moment of inflation (our first semireliable indication of temperature, ~10^{35} degrees Kelvin) and the moment after inflation (~10^{27} degrees Kelvin). The difference is roughly 100 decillion degrees Kelvin—orders of magnitude more than "a few nonillion degrees," but less pleasing on the page.

. . . really very teeny tiny. Quarky, to be exact The period immediately following inflation is called the Quark Epoch. This is because quarks—fundamental subatomic particles that act as the foundation for other, perhaps more familiar particles (protons, neutrons, etc.)—come into and out of existence. This span of time, between 10^{-32} seconds and 1 second after the Big Bang also sees the presence of other fundamental particles (e.g., electrons) and the formation of composite particles (e.g., protons and neutrons) from the interactions between the existing fundamental particles.

Luckily, this stuff you can't see is there only for a second For every quark there is an antiquark, for every proton an antiproton—and the same is true for all of the fundamental particles. What's fascinating about these matter/antimatter pairs is that they annihilate one another, and would have done so until the end of time unless a small asymmetry of matter dominated (for example, 100,000,001 particles of matter created for every 100,000,000 particles of antimatter). This must be the case, as otherwise we would not exist.

a boily, bubbly soup After 1 second has passed, the universe has entered a stage called nucleosynthesis, in which nuclei are formed. Nuclei (singular: nucleus) are the centers of atoms, composed of protons and neutrons, that give each kind of atom its distinctive character. Also at this stage, at and after 1 second, the annihilation of matter and antimatter and the interactions between other fundamental particles has generated photons—particles of electromagnetic radiation, such as light. However, because of the way the photons interact with the other particles, there is nowhere for this energy to go. This, in combination with the fact that there are no light-producing stars, means that the universe is opaque—a boily, bubbly particle soup.

Now turn the temperature down to Just Sorta Kinda Hot The universe continues to expand and cool. The temperature is now roughly 1 billion degrees Kelvin, and the time is around 100 seconds after the Big Bang.

That particle soup-sea-pond is about to stop bubbling and form atoms! 377,000 years after the Big Bang, the first atoms form. Scientists call this moment recombination, though it's a misnomer. In reality, the nuclei and electrons are combining to form atoms for the first time—mostly hydrogen and helium. Scientists predict that there would also be some lithium produced due to nucleosynthesis, but they don't observe as much as these predictions suggest. This so-called lithium abundance remains an open question. Whether it is hydrogen and helium, or hydrogen, helium and lithium, it is not until these first atoms form the first stars that any other new atoms (and therefore new elements) will be produced (more on this below).

That's all of your light escaping This refers to a point in the creation of the universe when all of the photons that had been bouncing around for the first 370,000 years could finally burst out of the confines of the young universe's particle soup. It is this light—called the cosmic microwave background, observable today as microwave radiation—that has taught us so much of what we know about the early universe. The reason we "see" this light as microwaves is because the once-visible-spectrum waves have redshifted over time—i.e., their wavelengths became longer due to the expansion of the universe.

Those atoms . . . will need some time to get to know one another For atoms to eventually form stars, first they need to come together into clouds of gas. During this period (between 370,000 years and 100–200 million years after the Big Bang) these clouds coalesce and collapse under their own gravity. They lack the critical mass—and, therefore, the gravity—to form stars.

That will allow the gas clouds to come together 180 million years after the Big Bang, as massive amounts of matter collect, the gas clouds form the first stars. The reason mass is important here is because an object's gravity is proportional to its mass. With enough mass present in the gas clouds, there is enough gravity to hold them together and overcome the pressures generated in the thermonuclear reactions that give birth to (and sustain) stars. Though there is more to be said about stars, one thing worth mentioning here is the synthesis of new elements inside stars. Without stars, we would only have hydrogen, helium and (perhaps) some lithium. Thanks to the high-energy nuclear reactions in their cores, though, we now have a whole slew of elements—ones that have been scattered across the universe and come to form the likes of water, breathable air, and organic life-forms (e.g., humans).

Your universe has a lot of gravity There is a lot of gravity in the universe, whether from black holes, stars, planets, moons—even you. It is the ever-present and invisible force that attracts objects to one another in proportion to their mass, and it is responsible for keeping our feet tethered to the earth, our earth tethered to the sun, and our sun tethered to the Milky Way—among many, many other things. It is impossible to say whether or not that means that when baking a universe, one is at risk of falling in—but gravity is certainly important in the cosmic landscape.

Universes are best experienced at room temperature Room temperature here refers to the length of time it took our universe to cool and expand into what we're living in today—roughly 13.8 billion years.

Your stars will come together and form swirly, spirally galaxies! Around 400 million years after the Big Bang the first galaxies formed—beautiful syntheses of stars, gaseous clouds, black holes, and lots and lots of gravity.

Planets will pop up The first planets are thought to have formed around 900 million years after the Big Bang, when matter (like gas and dust) came together around stars.

And there will be explosions. Big ones. This refers directly to supernovae—the spectacular and explosive deaths of massive stars that occur when they have burned through all of their available fuel sources. However, it also refers indirectly to the vast complexity of the universe. Cosmic explosions, collisions, and reactions happen on scales both unimaginably large and unimaginably small, and have since the universe's birth.

is *that your universe?* This references what scientists call the many worlds interpretation of quantum mechanics, which suggests that there are an infinite number of parallel worlds existing at the same space and time as our own. More than just fodder for science fiction, the many worlds interpretation is a useful way of explaining some of the problems astronomers and physicists observe in the birth of the universe and the fluctuating states of quantum particles. Unfortunately, if every possible outcome is taking place in some universe somewhere, there is no way of either proving or disproving this hypothesis —at least, not yet!

Particle Soup (Glossary)

Antimatter: For every particle of matter there is a particle of antimatter (or, an antiparticle) with the same mass but opposite charge. For example, the antiparticle of a proton (positively charged) is an antiproton (negatively charged).

Atom: Atoms are the units of matter that form elements. They are made up of smaller, subatomic particles, namely protons, neutrons, and electrons.

Composite particle: A composite particle is a particle that is made up of other, smaller fundamental particles (e.g., a proton is made up of three quarks).

Electron: Electrons are subatomic particles that carry a negative charge. In atoms, electrons orbit nuclei made up of protons and neutrons.

Element: An element is a substance made up of atoms that have the same numbers of protons in their nuclei. This number of protons determines what element it is: one proton is hydrogen, two is helium, three is lithium, etc.

Fundamental particle: A fundamental particle is a particle that cannot be broken down into other, smaller particles (e.g., quarks).

Neutron: Neutrons are subatomic particles that carry no electrical charge. They are present alongside protons in the nuclei of all atoms except hydrogen.

Nucleus (plural: **nuclei):** The nucleus is the dense core of an atom, formed out of a mixture of protons and neutrons.

Photon: Photons are fundamental particles without mass that make up the electromagnetic spectrum. This includes all radio waves, microwaves, infrared radiation, visible light, ultraviolet rays, X-rays, and gamma rays.

Proton: Protons are subatomic particles that carry a positive charge. They are present in every atomic nucleus.

Quark: Quarks are fundamental subatomic particles that combine to form composite particles, such as protons and neutrons.

Subatomic particle: Subatomic particle is a general term for a particle smaller than an atom. They can be *fundamental particles*, such as quarks, or *composite particles*, such as neutrons or protons.

Timeline

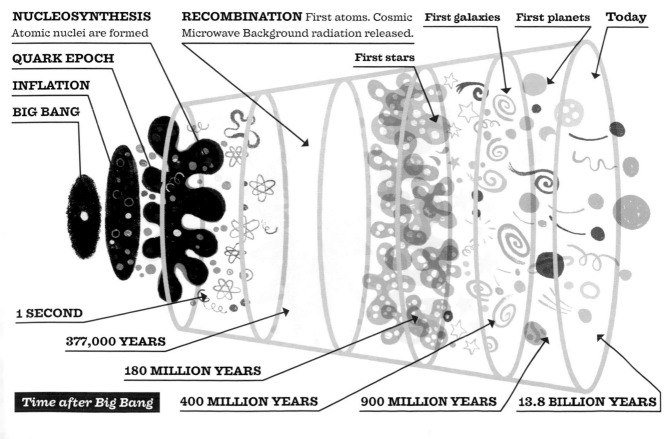

NUCLEOSYNTHESIS
Atomic nuclei are formed

RECOMBINATION First atoms. Cosmic Microwave Background radiation released.

First galaxies   **First planets**   **Today**

QUARK EPOCH

INFLATION

First stars

BIG BANG

1 SECOND

377,000 YEARS

180 MILLION YEARS

Time after Big Bang   **400 MILLION YEARS**   **900 MILLION YEARS**   **13.8 BILLION YEARS**

Acknowledgments

I'd like to extend my sincerest thanks to Simon Boughton, my editor, whose belief in *How to Bake a Universe* is the reason these pages now exist; Brian Biggs, the amazingly talented artist who took an outlandish vision and made it a reality; Tanusri Prasanna, my fearless agent and greatest ally in all things writing and publishing; Dr. Daniel Hoff, for keeping me tethered to the science (and whimsy!) in the ways only a real physicist, and genuine friend, could; and the scientific community at large, whose tireless dedication to discovery, stewardship, and pedagogy have provided us all with the tools to better understand ourselves in this wild and awe-inspiring universe.

I consulted many sources for this book, the most important being:

For all things astrophysics: **NASA Astrophysics (science.nasa.gov/astrophysics)**

For all things particle physics: **CERN (home.cern/science/physics/standard-model)**

A diagram of temperature vs. time was consulted for perspective, though it is dated most recently to 2004, and therefore not directly quoted in the text: Edward L. Wright, "Brief History of the Universe," UCLA Division of Astronomy & Astrophysics **(astro.ucla.edu/~wright/BBhistory.html)**